Anatomy of a PANDEMIC

by Amber J. Keyser

Consultant:
Marcia Lee
Department of Microbiology
Miami University
Oxford, Ohio

CAPSTONE PRESS
a capstone imprint

Velocity is published by Capstone Press,
151 Good Counsel Drive, P.O. Box 669, Mankato, Minnesota 56002.
www.capstonepub.com

Copyright © 2011 by Capstone Press, a Capstone imprint.
All rights reserved. No part of this publication may be reproduced in whole or in part, or stored in a retrieval system, or transmitted in any form or by any means, electronic, mechanical, photocopying, recording, or otherwise, without written permission of the publisher. For information regarding permission, write to Capstone Press, 151 Good Counsel Drive, P.O. Box 669, Dept. R, Mankato, Minnesota 56002.

 Books published by Capstone Press are manufactured with paper containing at least 10 percent post-consumer waste.

Library of Congress Cataloging-in-Publication Data
Anatomy of a pandemic / by Amber J. Keyser.
  p. cm.—(Velocity. Disasters.)
Includes bibliographical references and index.
Summary: "Describes pandemics, including the microbes that cause disease, what causes diseases to spread, and how scientists are working to stop pandemics"—Provided by publisher.
ISBN 978-1-4296-5493-7 (library binding)
ISBN 978-1-4296-6280-2 (paperback)
1. Epidemics—Juvenile literature. I. Title. II. Series.
RA653.5.K49 2011
614.4—dc22   2010027647

Editorial Credits
Carrie Braulick Sheely, editor; Alison Thiele, designer; Svetlana Zhurkin, media researcher; Laura Manthe, production specialist

Photo Credits
Alamy/Jake Lyell, 26–27; Alamy/Medical-on-Line, 11 (bottom); Alamy/North Wind Picture Archives, 7; Alamy/The Print Collector, 15 (bottom); Alamy/World History Archive, 12 (left); Artville, 13 (top); The Bridgeman Art Library/Private Collection/Archives Charmet, 13 (middle); Capstone Press, 5 (top), 31 (top), 35; Capstone Studio/Karon Dubke, cover (bottom middle), 4–5 (bottom), 16 (left), 42 (bottom); CDC, 11 (top), 19 (right and top left), 21 (right and bottom left), 23 (bottom), 24–25 (back); CDC/Dan Higgins, 20; CDC/Frederick Murphy, 21 (top left); CDC/James Gathany, 13 (bottom), 22 (bottom), 31 (bottom), 37 (bottom, all); CDC/Janice Haney Carr, 16–17 (back), 19 (bottom left), 22 (top), 43 (top and middle); CDC/John Montenieri, 24 (bottom); Comstock, 44 (top left, middle right, and bottom); Corbis/Bettmann, 14; Corbis/Royalty-free, 40–41 (back); Creatas, 44 (middle left); Franklin D. Roosevelt Library/Margaret Suckley, 9; Getty Images/3D4Medical, 29 (left); Getty Images/Liaison/Paula Bronstein, 23 (top); Getty Images/Three Lions, 15 (top); iStockphoto/Bart Coenders, 30; iStockphoto/Christopher Badzioch, 40 (middle); iStockphoto/Evelyn Peyton, 45 (top); iStockphoto/Jonathan Heger, 41 (top); iStockphoto/Michael Krinke, 36 (bottom); iStockphoto/Mikhail Kokhanchikov, 42 (top); iStockphoto/Natthawat Wongrat, 25 (top); iStockphoto/Tom Begasse, 37 (top); Library of Congress, 8, 16 (right), 17; Newscom, 34; Newscom/AFP/FBI, 33; Photolibrary/Marcia Hartsock, 18–19; Purestock, 28–29 (back), 28 (top); Shutterstock/Andrea Danti, 29 (right); Shutterstock/Bryan Busovicki, 12 (right); Shutterstock/Donald R. Swartz, cover (bottom left), 45 (bottom right); Shutterstock/Hinochika, 36–37 (back); Shutterstock/Nikonov (metal background), throughout; Shutterstock/Oculo (mosaic design element), cover and throughout; Shutterstock/Pavel Losevsky, 38–39; Shutterstock/Peter Dean, 4 (top); Shutterstock/Peter Grosch, 25 (bottom); Shutterstock/Rob Byron, cover (top); Shutterstock/Sebastian Kaulitzki (scratched metal background), back cover and throughout, 10–11 (back); Shutterstock/Stanislav E. Petrov (cement background), throughout; Shutterstock/swissmacky, 43 (bottom); Visuals Unlimited/Dennis Kunkel Microscopy, 23 (middle); Wikipedia, 32

Printed in the United States of America in Stevens Point, Wisconsin.
092010   005934WZS11

TABLE OF CONTENTS

Introduction: Sick Days   4

Chapter 1: Hideous History   6

Chapter 2: The Amazing World of Microbes   14

Chapter 3: Attack and Defense   24

Chapter 4: Tracking Pandemics   30

Chapter 5: Looking to the Future   38

    Glossary   46
    Read More   47
    Internet Sites   47
    Index   48

Introduction

SICK DAYS

Your head throbs. Your body aches. Chills sweep over you one after another. Between the chills, you break out in sweats. There's no doubt about it—you're sick. You've been infected by a tiny living thing called a **microbe**. And if the disease is infectious, sometimes you can spread it to others.

Not that it's a big deal. People get sick all the time. They stay home from school or work for a few days. Then they feel better. The occasional cold or flu is a normal part of everyday life.

But what if half your math class is out sick? Or what if local hospitals are overwhelmed with people reporting the same **symptoms**? In these cases, your community may be experiencing a higher than normal rate of an infectious disease, or an outbreak.

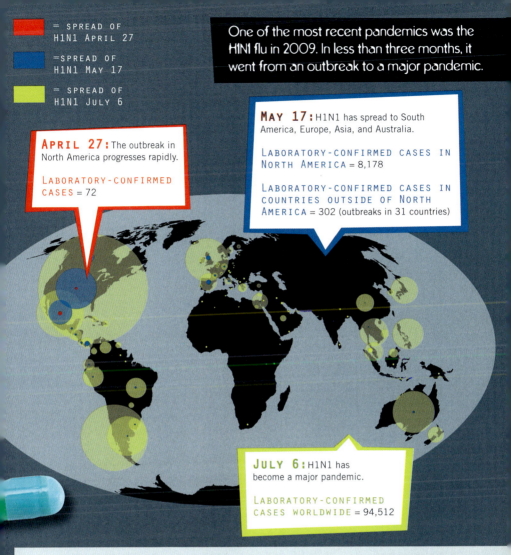

■ = SPREAD OF H1N1 APRIL 27
■ = SPREAD OF H1N1 MAY 17
■ = SPREAD OF H1N1 JULY 6

One of the most recent pandemics was the H1N1 flu in 2009. In less than three months, it went from an outbreak to a major pandemic.

APRIL 27: The outbreak in North America progresses rapidly.
LABORATORY-CONFIRMED CASES = 72

MAY 17: H1N1 has spread to South America, Europe, Asia, and Australia.
LABORATORY-CONFIRMED CASES IN NORTH AMERICA = 8,178
LABORATORY-CONFIRMED CASES IN COUNTRIES OUTSIDE OF NORTH AMERICA = 302 (outbreaks in 31 countries)

JULY 6: H1N1 has become a major pandemic.
LABORATORY-CONFIRMED CASES WORLDWIDE = 94,512

An epidemic is underway if the outbreak affects a large number of people at the same time. At this point, the outbreak has spread. But it is limited to a relatively small area, such as a state.

If the disease continues to spread, a pandemic can occur. A pandemic occurs when the epidemic affects people over a very wide area. Pandemics usually affect a whole continent or several continents.

microbe—a tiny living thing too small to be seen without a microscope; microbes are also called microorganisms, and disease-causing microbes are sometimes called germs

symptom—a sign of an illness

Chapter 1

HIDEOUS HISTORY

Today pandemics like the 2009 H1N1 make big headlines. But pandemics are nothing new. They've been causing worldwide misery and death since ancient times.

APPROXIMATE YEARS	DISEASE	WHAT'S THE STORY?
? BC–present	malaria	One of the first written reports of malaria is from 2700 BC. Today malaria is mainly confined to Africa. But the disease also often occurs in northern South America and in southern Asia. The disease kills more than 1 million people each year.
early 540s–mid-700s	bubonic plague	Several bubonic plague pandemics sweep through Europe. The first occurs between 541 and 544. This outbreak started in Egypt. Then it spread to southern Europe. People died so quickly from the bubonic plague that they often wore name tags when they left their homes. That way, their bodies could be identified if they died.
early 1300s–late 1300s	bubonic plague	Once again, a bubonic plague pandemic spreads through Europe. By 1400 the disease kills more than 20 million people. The pandemic earns the name Black Death because victims develop black spots all over their bodies.

APPROXIMATE YEARS	DISEASE	WHAT'S THE STORY?
1520s–late 1500s	typhus	Typhus spreads throughout Europe. It is often called camp fever or ship fever because it easily spreads in crowded living spaces.
Late 1610s–mid-1800s	smallpox	Smallpox pandemics affect Europe, Asia, Africa, and North America. Nine out of 10 American Indians in some tribes die from smallpox in North America. In England, 9 out of 10 smallpox deaths between 1780 and 1800 are young children.

APPROXIMATE YEARS	DISEASE	WHAT'S THE STORY?
Late 1810s–mid-1820s	cholera	A cholera pandemic strikes Asia, infecting hundreds of thousands of people. Some people believe the cold winter of 1823–1824 stopped further spread of the disease.
1894–1904	bubonic plague	A bubonic plague pandemic starts in Asia and spreads around the world. Infected sailors rapidly spread the disease to others when they arrive in harbor towns.
1899–early 1920s	cholera	A cholera pandemic again breaks out in Asia. In India the pandemic kills more than 800,000 people. It later spreads to northern Africa, Russia, and parts of Europe.
1918–1919	Spanish flu	The Spanish flu pandemic affects the world, killing about 50 million people. About one-fifth of the world's population is infected. At least 600,000 people in the United States die of the disease.

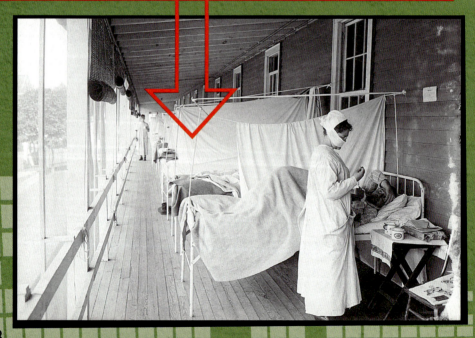

APPROXIMATE YEARS	DISEASE	WHAT'S THE STORY?
1942–1953	polio	A polio pandemic occurs in the United States and Western Europe. In 1952 more than 600,000 cases are reported worldwide. By the mid-1950s, **vaccinations** bring the **virus** under control in most countries.
1961–	cholera	Even today, a lack of safe drinking water has led to cholera pandemics. In 1961 a cholera outbreak starts in South Asia. It then reaches Africa and spreads to North and South America. According to the World Health Organization (WHO), the pandemic continues.

FRANKLIN D. ROOSEVELT'S SECRET

Franklin D. Roosevelt, the 32nd U.S. president, survived polio as a young man. It left him disabled, and he was forced to use a wheelchair. However, few Americans knew this fact about their president. Roosevelt worked hard to keep the wheelchair from being seen. He didn't allow photographers to show it in pictures. Only two photos of Roosevelt in his wheelchair are known to exist.

vaccination—a shot of dead or weakened germs injected into a person or animal to provide protection against a virus; the dead or weakened germ is called a vaccine

virus—a microorganism with a simple structure that depends on infecting other cells to reproduce

Symptoms of Disease

Doctors identify diseases based on their patients' symptoms. In a pandemic, all the victims show similar symptoms.

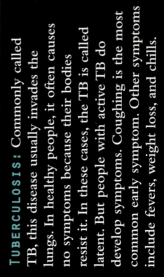

INFLUENZA: Almost everybody knows what the flu feels like. Headaches, body aches, and cycles of fever and chills are common. Those infected also may feel weak and have a sore throat. Flu is most dangerous when the flu-weakened immune system can't fight off other infections.

TUBERCULOSIS: Commonly called TB, this disease usually invades the lungs. In healthy people, it often causes no symptoms because their bodies resist it. In these cases, the TB is called latent. But people with active TB do develop symptoms. Coughing is the most common early symptom. Other symptoms include fevers, weight loss, and chills.

POLIO: This virus attacks the nervous system. Non-paralytic polio symptoms include fever, headaches, and sore throats. Paralytic polio is more serious and can lead to paralysis. Symptoms of this polio type include severe muscle aches and floppy limbs on one side of the body.

TYPHUS: Typhus often causes a high fever and a skin rash. Headaches and muscle pain are other common symptoms. It can progress to brain swelling and death.

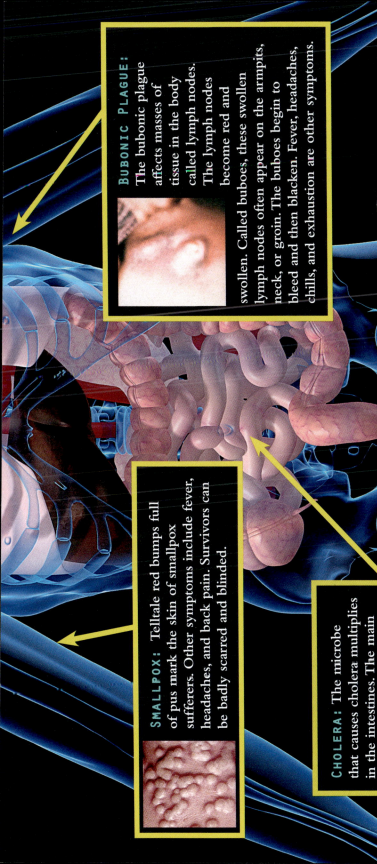

BUBONIC PLAGUE: The bubonic plague affects masses of tissue in the body called lymph nodes. The lymph nodes become red and swollen. Called buboes, these swollen lymph nodes often appear on the armpits, neck, or groin. The buboes begin to bleed and then blacken. Fever, headaches, chills, and exhaustion are other symptoms.

dehydration—a life-threatening medical condition caused by a lack of water

SMALLPOX: Telltale red bumps full of pus mark the skin of smallpox sufferers. Other symptoms include fever, headaches, and back pain. Survivors can be badly scarred and blinded.

CHOLERA: The microbe that causes cholera multiplies in the intestines. The main symptom is severe diarrhea. Patients can die within hours from **dehydration**.

Evil Curses and Unusual Cures

Hundreds of years ago, people didn't know that microbes cause disease. But early cultures did develop their own ideas about disease causes and cures.

Many people of ancient times believed that diseases were sent by evil spirits. These beliefs were also present in more recent times. In the late 1800s, many Americans believed tuberculosis turned people into vampires. They thought vampires then spread the disease to others.

People around the world believed bubonic plague was a punishment from the gods. People punished themselves by hitting their bodies with whips or sticks. They hoped the punishment would earn forgiveness from the gods.

In the 1820s, cholera hit Thailand. The king promised that he could cure the sick. How? He ordered that the Emerald Buddha statue be carried in a procession through the crowds of sick citizens.

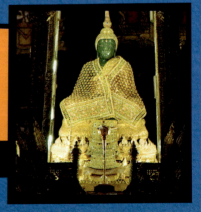

Emerald Buddha

Tuberculosis was called the "king's evil" in England and France in the 1700s. People believed they would be cured if a king touched them.

As late as the 1600s, smallpox sufferers in Europe practiced heat therapy. They bundled in blankets and huddled near fires. Europeans also practiced red therapy. They wore only red clothing and ate only red food. People treating them used only red medical tools.

In the 400s BC, people in ancient Greece thought the human body contained four "humors." They were phlegm, blood, black bile, and yellow bile. People thought imbalanced humors caused disease. Belief in the four humors continued through the Middle Ages (about AD 400–1500) in Europe. To balance the blood humor, people practiced bloodletting. Doctors used leeches to suck blood from patients' bodies or made small cuts in the arms to drain "excess" blood. To balance the bile humor, people drank herbal mixtures that caused vomiting or diarrhea.

Many cultures worshipped a god or goddess who they believed could cure smallpox. In India it was Shitala Mata. In China prayers went to T'ou-Shen Niang-Niang. And in West Africa, people prayed to Shapona.

Shapona statue

"Ring around the rosy, a pocketful of posies. Ashes, ashes, we all fall down!" You probably know these lyrics to the children's song "Ring around the Rosy." This song may sound sweet, but it's really about the bubonic plague. The sick had rose-colored markings. Survivors carried flowers to cover up the smell of the dead and dying.

Chapter 2

THE AMAZING WORLD OF MICROBES

So if disease isn't caused by evil spirits or imbalanced humors, what makes people sick? Before you run off shouting, "Cooties!," meet the people who helped uncover the world of microbes.

Anton van Leeuwenhoek (1632–1723)

Anton van Leeuwenhoek was a cloth merchant with a curious streak. In the late 1600s, he built more than 400 magnifying devices, originally to inspect cloth. These "microscopes" allowed Leeuwenhoek to see objects more than 200 times their actual size. He soon used the devices to examine pond water, tooth plaque, and almost anything else he could find. Through his devices, he discovered microbes no one had ever seen before. People were shocked to see the tiny "animalcules." Leeuwenhoek's discoveries helped open the door to understanding the causes of disease.

Edward Jenner (1749–1823)

In the late 1700s, Europeans lived in fear of getting smallpox. In Great Britain, farmers noticed that those who recovered from cowpox never seemed to get smallpox. Cowpox was a common illness similar to smallpox, but it was much less deadly. The farmers' observations gave doctor Edward Jenner an idea. In 1796 he rubbed pus from a cowpox sore into a small cut in the skin of a young boy. This vaccination protected the boy from smallpox. Suddenly there was hope that the "speckled monster" could be stopped. Thanks to Jenner's vaccine, smallpox is gone. The last natural case occurred in 1977. However, a few samples of the smallpox virus survive in laboratories for use in research.

Edward Jenner giving vaccination that controlled the spread of smallpox

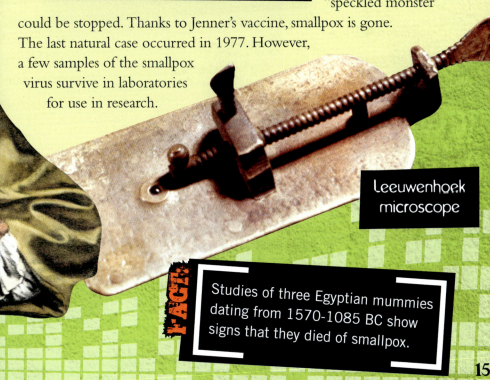

Leeuwenhoek microscope

FACT: Studies of three Egyptian mummies dating from 1570-1085 BC show signs that they died of smallpox.

Louis Pasteur (1822–1895)

Three of Louis Pasteur's five children died of typhoid fever. If anyone was motivated to understand microbes, he was. Pasteur's experiments proved that microbes cause disease. Pasteur also developed several vaccines.

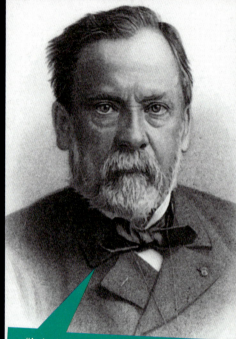

"It is in the power of man to make parasitic maladies disappear from the face of the globe!"
—LOUIS PASTEUR

In the early 1860s, Pasteur showed that microbes could be killed by heat. Check your milk carton. It will say "pasteurized." Thanks to Pasteur's work, the milk is not going to make you sick.

FACT: In 1898 Dr. Paul-Louis Simond discovered that the microbe that causes bubonic plague is carried from rats to people by fleas. This discovery led to better control of the disease. But when he first released his findings, many other scientists refused to believe him.

the microbes that cause anthrax

Robert Koch (1843–1910)

Robert Koch identified the microbes that cause tuberculosis, cholera, and anthrax. Plus he laid out the four rules for knowing whether a microbe caused a certain disease. Today these rules are known as Koch's postulates. Through Koch's work, scientists have been able to find the causes of most major diseases.

KOCH'S POSTULATES

1. The microbe must exist in every case of the disease.

2. The microbe must be separated from the diseased animal. The microbe also must be able to be grown in a laboratory.

3. The grown microbe, when put into a healthy animal, must cause the animal to show symptoms of infection.

4. The microbe must be recoverable from the newly infected animal. In doing so, the same microbe as the one believed to cause the disease must be found.

The work of Leeuwenhoek, Jenner, Pasteur, Koch, and others helped people begin to understand disease. Over the years, many scientists have built on the work of these pioneers. Today we know that most diseases are caused by three kinds of microbes—**bacteria**, viruses, and **protozoans**.

Bacteria

Bacteria should get some kind of award. They are everywhere in uncountable numbers. From hot deserts to the deep sea, bacteria thrive. They do thousands of different jobs. But don't worry—not all bacteria cause disease. In fact, some bacteria are helpful. Bacteria break down dead plants and animals. Without bacteria, we couldn't make cheese or bread. We would die without vitamin K produced by bacteria in our intestines. And digesting our food? It would be very difficult without help from bacteria.

Nearly all bacteria are surrounded by a cell wall. The wall provides structure to the cell. A molecule called peptidoglycan keeps the cell wall rigid. It also helps the bacterium reproduce.

Each bacterium is filled with a jellylike substance called cytoplasm. The cytoplasm helps break down food.

Many bacteria have stringlike flagella that help the cell move.

One long strand of **DNA** floats in the center of the cell like tangled string.

caused by *Yersinia pestis*

DISEASES CAUSED BY BACTERIA:

- ANTHRAX
- BUBONIC PLAGUE
- CHOLERA
- LEPROSY
- LYME DISEASE
- SALMONELLOSIS
- TUBERCULOSIS
- TYPHOID FEVER
- TYPHUS

caused by *Borrelia burgdorferi*

caused by *Salmonella*

FACT! Bacteria are grouped according to their shapes. Round bacteria are called cocci. Rod-shaped bacteria are bacilli. Spiral-shaped bacteria are either spirilla or spirochetes.

Some bacteria have pili, which look similar to flagella. Pili help a bacterium attach to another bacterium.

bacterium—a one-celled, microscopic organism; bacteria exist in and on all living things

protozoan—a single-celled organism that has at least one nucleus; protozoans can be animal-like or plantlike

DNA—the molecule that carries all of the instructions to make a living thing and keep it working; DNA stands for deoxyribonucleic acid

Viruses

Most viruses are smaller than bacteria. Millions of viruses could fit on a pinhead. But don't be fooled by their small size—viruses cause many deadly diseases. As far as structure, there's not much to a virus. Each one has either DNA or RNA enclosed in a protein shell called a capsid. Some have surface proteins or a membrane envelope on the outside. These extra features help the virus invade.

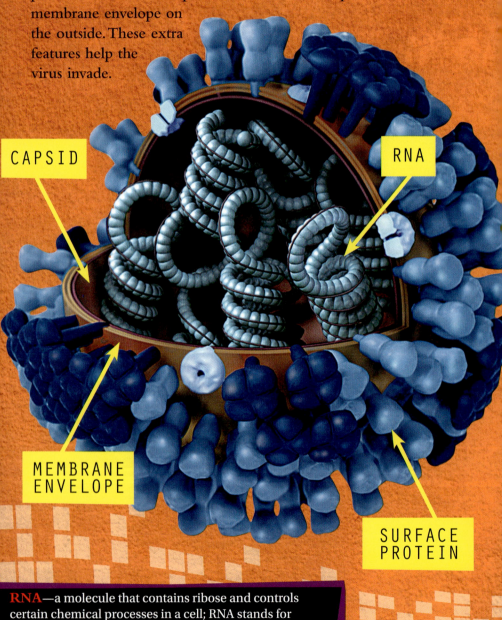

CAPSID

RNA

MEMBRANE ENVELOPE

SURFACE PROTEIN

RNA—a molecule that contains ribose and controls certain chemical processes in a cell; RNA stands for ribonucleic acid

And invading is what viruses do! Viruses can't reproduce on their own. Instead, they infect cells and put them to work.

1. First, the virus forces the infected cell, or host cell, to make virus copies. The infected cell fills with more viruses.

2. Eventually, the cell explodes, spewing out the viruses.

3. These viruses then infect new cells. In this way, a viral infection spreads in the body.

DISEASES CAUSED BY VIRUSES:

- COLDS
- DENGUE
- EBOLA HEMORRHAGIC FEVER
- FLU
- HEPATITIS (VIRAL FORMS)
- HERPES
- HIV/AIDS
- POLIO
- RABIES
- SMALLPOX

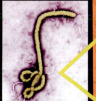
caused by Ebola virus

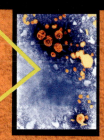
caused by Hepatitis virus, either A, B (shown), C, D, or E

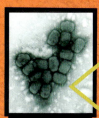
caused by Variola virus

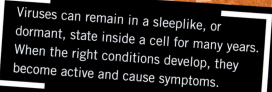

FACT: Viruses can remain in a sleeplike, or dormant, state inside a cell for many years. When the right conditions develop, they become active and cause symptoms.

Protozoans

Protozoans come in a variety of shapes and colors. Some are like animals that move around looking for things to eat. Others are like plants. These plantlike protozoans use energy from the sun to make their own food. Eating plantlike protozoans doesn't cause sickness. However, some animal-like protozoans are parasites, and these are the troublemakers. When they live inside the body, they can cause disease.

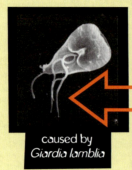

caused by *Giardia lamblia*

DISEASES CAUSED BY PROTOZOANS:

- AFRICAN SLEEPING SICKNESS
- DYSENTERY
- GIARDIASIS
- LEISHMANIASIS
- MALARIA
- TOXOPLASMOSIS

How Malaria Spreads and Attacks

Malaria is caused by protozoan parasites called plasmodia. Plasmodia live part of their life cycle in human blood and the other part in a mosquito. The mosquito is called a vector because it transfers the parasite from one person to another.

2. Inside the mosquito, the plasmodia form sporozoites. These are like seeds ready to infect another person. The sporozoites eventually move to the mosquito's salivary glands.

1. When a mosquito bites a person with malaria, plasmodia are sucked up with the blood meal.

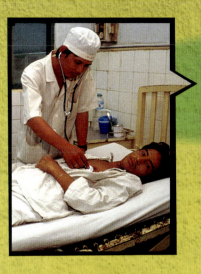

6. Each plasmodium divides to make hundreds of copies of itself. When the red blood cell is jammed full, it explodes. The explosion releases more plasmodia into the bloodstream. These plasmodia invade more cells, creating a cycle. The cycles of attack on the red blood cells cause fever, chills, and pain. If a mosquito bites the infected person, the cycle starts again.

5. Each round plasmodium enters a red blood cell.

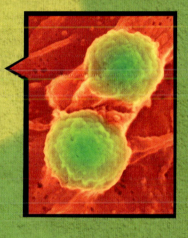

4. The sporozoites enter liver cells, where they develop into a round form. In this form, plasmodia can invade blood cells.

3. When the mosquito bites an uninfected person, the sporozoites in its saliva are shot into the blood.

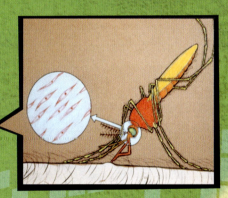

Only female mosquitoes dine on blood. They need the blood to help their eggs develop.

Chapter 3

ATTACK AND DEFENSE

Transmission

To cause a pandemic, microbes must move directly from person to person or indirectly through water, food, or animal bites. That's called transmission. Some microbes are more easily spread, or contagious, than others. Very contagious microbes are more likely to cause a pandemic. Here are some common ways microbes are transmitted.

AIR: When a sick person sneezes or coughs, droplets filled with viruses or bacteria spew through the air. Look out! If you're in range, you might get sick.

ANIMALS/VECTORS: Diseases can spread when saliva from infected animals enters the body through animal bites. Rabies can spread in this way. Malaria and yellow fever are transmitted when disease-infected mosquitoes feed on humans. Fleas are vectors of bubonic plague.

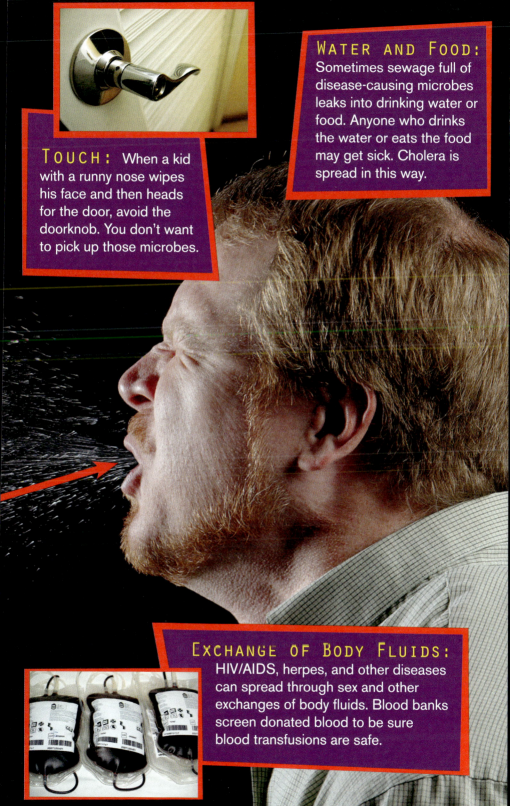

TOUCH: When a kid with a runny nose wipes his face and then heads for the door, avoid the doorknob. You don't want to pick up those microbes.

WATER AND FOOD: Sometimes sewage full of disease-causing microbes leaks into drinking water or food. Anyone who drinks the water or eats the food may get sick. Cholera is spread in this way.

EXCHANGE OF BODY FLUIDS: HIV/AIDS, herpes, and other diseases can spread through sex and other exchanges of body fluids. Blood banks screen donated blood to be sure blood transfusions are safe.

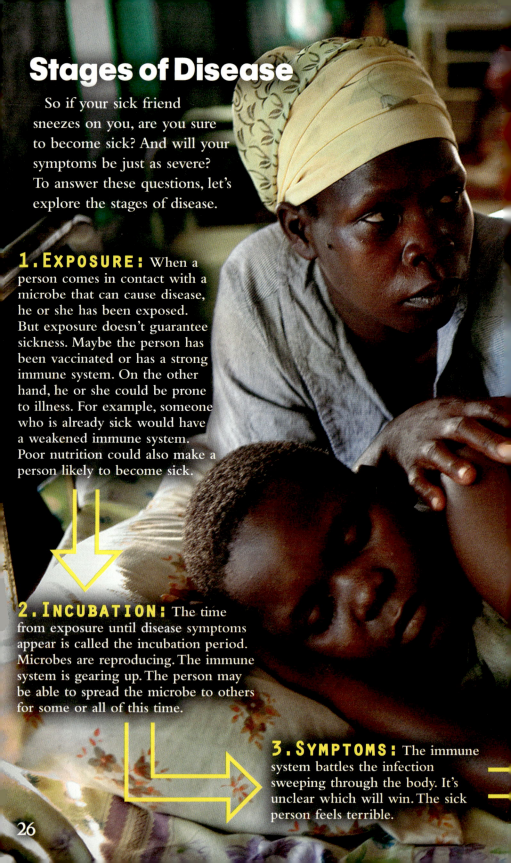

Stages of Disease

So if your sick friend sneezes on you, are you sure to become sick? And will your symptoms be just as severe? To answer these questions, let's explore the stages of disease.

1. EXPOSURE: When a person comes in contact with a microbe that can cause disease, he or she has been exposed. But exposure doesn't guarantee sickness. Maybe the person has been vaccinated or has a strong immune system. On the other hand, he or she could be prone to illness. For example, someone who is already sick would have a weakened immune system. Poor nutrition could also make a person likely to become sick.

2. INCUBATION: The time from exposure until disease symptoms appear is called the incubation period. Microbes are reproducing. The immune system is gearing up. The person may be able to spread the microbe to others for some or all of this time.

3. SYMPTOMS: The immune system battles the infection sweeping through the body. It's unclear which will win. The sick person feels terrible.

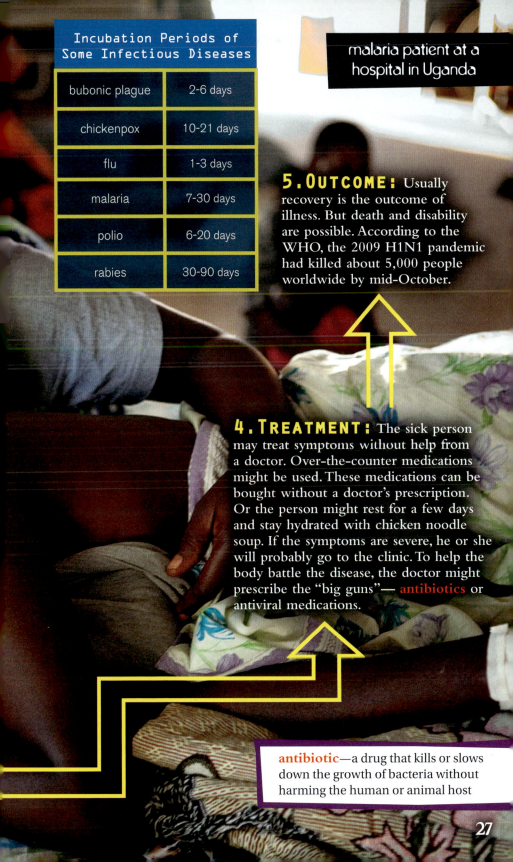

Incubation Periods of Some Infectious Diseases

bubonic plague	2-6 days
chickenpox	10-21 days
flu	1-3 days
malaria	7-30 days
polio	6-20 days
rabies	30-90 days

malaria patient at a hospital in Uganda

5. OUTCOME: Usually recovery is the outcome of illness. But death and disability are possible. According to the WHO, the 2009 H1N1 pandemic had killed about 5,000 people worldwide by mid-October.

4. TREATMENT: The sick person may treat symptoms without help from a doctor. Over-the-counter medications might be used. These medications can be bought without a doctor's prescription. Or the person might rest for a few days and stay hydrated with chicken noodle soup. If the symptoms are severe, he or she will probably go to the clinic. To help the body battle the disease, the doctor might prescribe the "big guns"— antibiotics or antiviral medications.

antibiotic—a drug that kills or slows down the growth of bacteria without harming the human or animal host

Body Defenses

With so many microbes surrounding you, it might seem that you are doomed for sickness. But our bodies have built-in defenses that help keep us healthy.

MUCOUS MEMBRANES: Gummy snot, or mucous, traps microbes that could cause trouble.

PHAGOCYTES: These white blood cells constantly patrol the blood and tissues for microbes. When they catch one, they swallow it whole.

white blood cells

SALIVA: Antibodies and other chemicals in saliva can kill some microbes.

GAG AND COUGH REFLEX: Coughing helps to eject microbes. But be sure to cough into your sleeve. Otherwise, the microbes could get into the air and infect others.

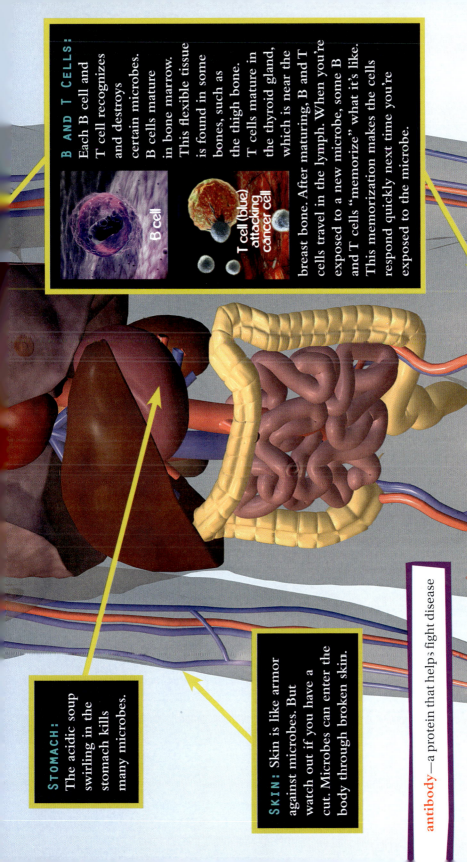

B AND T CELLS:
Each B cell and T cell recognizes and destroys certain microbes. B cells mature in bone marrow. This flexible tissue is found in some bones, such as the thigh bone. T cells mature in the thyroid gland, which is near the breast bone. After maturing, B and T cells travel in the lymph. When you're exposed to a new microbe, some B and T cells "memorize" what it's like. This memorization makes the cells respond quickly next time you're exposed to the microbe.

B cell

T cell (blue) attacking cancer cell

STOMACH:
The acidic soup swirling in the stomach kills many microbes.

SKIN:
Skin is like armor against microbes. But watch out if you have a cut. Microbes can enter the body through broken skin.

antibody—a protein that helps fight disease

Chapter 4

TRACKING PANDEMICS

It Takes Teamwork!

Doctors and nurses help maintain good public health by treating patients and teaching them how to stay healthy. But understanding and stopping a pandemic takes many more people. From scientists to homeland security officials, everyone has an important job.

Doctors

Doctors keep track of the number of people they see with similar symptoms. Every disease occurs at a normal level. When the number of cases jumps above that level, an epidemic may be on the way.

Ecologists

Ecologists study the relationship between animals and their environment. Some ecologists study animals that spread disease-causing microbes. These scientists examine environmental changes that could increase the risk of a pandemic occurring. For example, a large amount of rainfall could lead to a high mosquito population. The risk of a malaria pandemic could then increase.

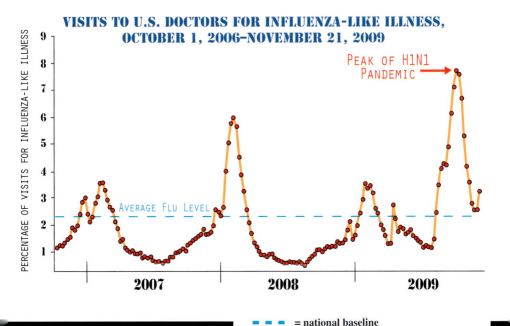

MICROBIOLOGISTS

Microbiologists study microscopic organisms such as bacteria and protozoans. Along with microbe structure and growth, they study the conditions that cause microbes to spread. The work of microbiologists helps scientists design new medications.

VIROLOGISTS

Virologists are microbiologists who study only viruses. These scientists try to predict how disease-causing viruses might change over time. The results of their studies are used to make new vaccines. These new vaccines could help keep a pandemic from spreading.

A microbiologist studies a reconstructed sample of the 1918 pandemic flu virus to understand why it became so deadly.

Epidemiologists

Epidemiologists are disease detectives. It's their job to find out how a disease spreads and how to prevent its further spread. Epidemiologists study patterns in how people are becoming infected. They consider where the sick people live and what their recent activities have been. Public health officials use the epidemiology reports when making announcements about how to prevent illness.

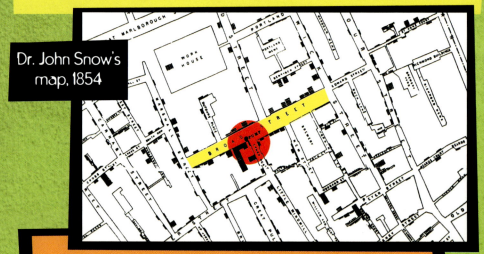

Dr. John Snow's map, 1854

DR. JOHN SNOW'S DISCOVERY

The first epidemiologist was Dr. John Snow. His good detective work stopped a cholera outbreak in 1854. The Golden Square neighborhood of London, England, was hit hard by this disease. People got sick and died within days or even hours. Dr. Snow tracked the deaths on a map. Each line stood for one person who had died at that address. He could see that most deaths clustered around the water pump on Broad Street. Ah-ha! He concluded that the water there was contaminated with the cholera bacterium. After the pump was shut down, the outbreak was controlled.

Environmental Scientists

When disease-causing microbes infect the air, water, or soil, environmental scientists go to work. They study the relationship between these microbes and the environment. Their job is to make the environment safe for humans. They may test and treat drinking water or find ways to purify indoor air.

U.S. Department of Homeland Security

In 1346 the Mongol army was attacking the walled city of Caffa. The Mongols were forced to retreat after being struck by the bubonic plague. But before they left, they catapulted rotting bodies into the city. In doing so, they spread plague to the people inside. This event is an example of **bioterrorism**. A bioterrorism attack could cause an epidemic or a pandemic. The U.S. Department of Homeland Security keeps track of terrorism risk. It also **puts bioterrorism response plans in place.**

In 2001 a bioterrorist sent letters laced with the bacterium that causes anthrax to senators and journalists. Five people died.

bioterrorism—a terrorism attack involving the use of bacteria, viruses, or other disease-causing organisms

CDC and WHO

U.S. doctors, public health workers, and medical scientists work closely with the Centers for Disease Control and Prevention (CDC) and the World Health Organization.

CDC

The CDC is dedicated to improving public health in the United States. Scientists track disease outbreaks and research cures. Educators promote healthy living. Medical experts from the CDC often speak to government leaders. Their advice helps lawmakers draft new laws that will help keep U.S. citizens healthy.

WHO

The WHO works to improve public health around the globe. WHO workers in every country distribute medicine, teach people how to stay healthy, and monitor patterns of disease. Most countries report cases of infectious disease to the WHO. These reports help scientists track the spread of epidemics and pandemics.

WHO director Margaret Chan spoke to the World Health Assembly in May 2009 about ways to fight the H1N1 flu.

The CDC and WHO share data and work closely together. They also use a similar six-phase alert system to notify the public about the threat of disease.

WHO LEVELS OF PANDEMIC ALERT

Phase 1: An animal infection could possibly move to humans.

Phase 2: An infection only seen before in animals has caused a few cases of infection in humans.

Phase 3: There are a few small clusters of disease in people.

Phase 4: Human-to-human transmission is known. The transmission leads to community-level disease outbreaks.

Phase 5: Disease spreads to at least two countries in one WHO region. A pandemic is very likely to happen soon.

Phase 6 (Pandemic Stage): Community-level outbreaks occur in at least one other country in a different WHO region from the one indicated in the phase 5 alert. Disease transmission occurs rapidly in both neighboring and separated countries. A pandemic is underway.

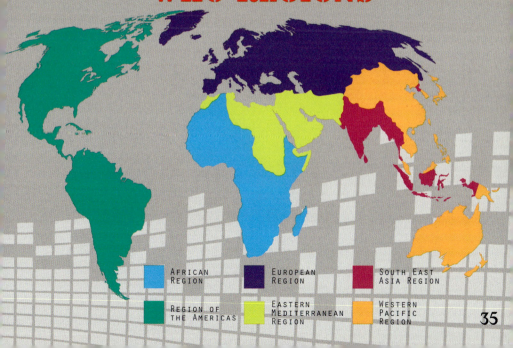

WHO REGIONS

- African Region
- Region of the Americas
- European Region
- Eastern Mediterranean Region
- South East Asia Region
- Western Pacific Region

Response Plans

No matter what type of infection causes a pandemic, response plans are in place for each alert level. During the first three pandemic alert phases, public health workers closely track the spread of disease. They prepare for the possibility that the disease will spread.

During the last three alert levels, public health workers respond quickly to stop the spread of disease. At this point, responses may include encouraging practices such as:

USE OF FACE MASKS: The use of face masks can help prevent the spread of disease through the air. Many people wore face masks during the 2003 outbreak of SARS (Severe Acute Respiratory Syndrome) and the 2009 H1N1 pandemic.

HAND WASHING: Frequent hand washing makes it less likely that germs will be transferred to others through touch.

SOCIAL DISTANCING: People might be encouraged to keep their distance from others. This could mean avoiding touching others.

BUILDING CLOSURES: Recommendations might be made to close schools and other places where people gather in large groups.

BOILING WATER: Heat kills most microbes. Boiling water for at least three minutes makes it safe to drink. In the United States, cities regularly test the water supply. If dangerous microbes were found, public service announcements might warn people to boil water to prevent illness.

ISOLATION OF SICK PEOPLE: Those who are sick might be encouraged to stay home to reduce the risk of disease transmission.

INCREASING THE AVAILABILITY OF MEDICATIONS: More antiviral or antibiotic drugs can be distributed to hospitals and clinics.

VACCINE DEVELOPMENT: Scientists might be asked to develop and distribute vaccines that target a new disease type, or strain. Scientists began working on a vaccine for the H1N1 flu in May 2009.

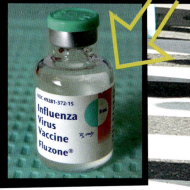

Chapter 5

LOOKING TO THE FUTURE

World Travelers

Throughout history, many infectious diseases have spread when people traveled. In AD 542, sick people on merchant ships carried bubonic plague from Egypt to Europe. In 1918 U.S. soldiers infected with the Spanish flu went to war in Europe. By doing so, the flu pandemic spread.

Today the world is more connected than ever before. Every day, airplanes, boats, trains, and trucks carry people and food from country to country. Microbes travel with us. This connectivity increases the chances that a pandemic will occur.

However, our global connections also provide ways to stop disease. Sharing information about outbreaks allows countries to work together to prevent pandemics. Media announcements give people a chance to protect themselves. In 2009 media reported that contaminated peanut butter was recalled. The announcement helped prevent the further spread of illness.

Becoming aware of tragedies such as pandemics also inspires people to help victims. For example, some organizations send medications to Africa to help HIV/AIDS patients. Other organizations build wells in countries that lack clean drinking water to prevent cholera outbreaks.

FACT: According to the WHO, about 884 million people did not have improved sources of drinking water in 2008. An improved source is one that protects the water from contamination.

Animal Alert!

People aren't just connected with other people. They're also in close contact with animals. Contact with animals can increase the chances of a pandemic occurring for several reasons.

Global warming has allowed mosquitoes to move into areas that used to be too cold for them. This expanded living area increases the risk of a pandemic occurring from a mosquito-borne disease.

PRIONS

While most diseases are caused by microbes, there are some rare diseases caused by prions. Most scientists think prions cause normal brain proteins to warp out of shape. When the abnormal protein hits a normal protein, the normal one warps too. One protein after another changes until brain function is destroyed. Eventually, the infected person dies.

Prion disease can spread between people and animals. In the early 1900s, an epidemic of a prion disease broke out among the Fore tribe of Papua New Guinea. This tribe honored its dead by eating the brains of dead tribal members. In this way, prions were passed from one person to another.

Cutting down forests and strip mining leaves standing water that creates new places for disease-carrying insects to live.

Growing cities are expanding into rural areas. Wild animals are then forced into closer contact with people. The shared living areas can lead to the spread of diseases carried by animals.

Large-scale production of animals for food means an increased chance that animal infections will jump to humans.

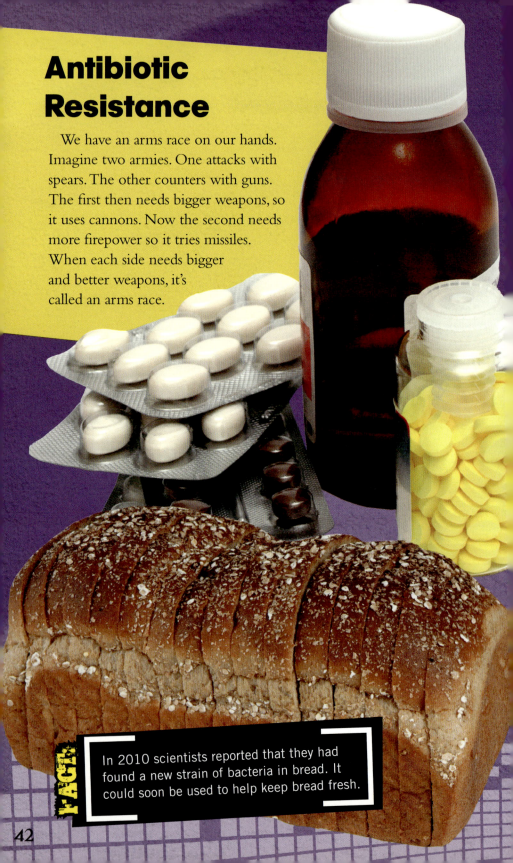

Antibiotic Resistance

We have an arms race on our hands. Imagine two armies. One attacks with spears. The other counters with guns. The first then needs bigger weapons, so it uses cannons. Now the second needs more firepower so it tries missiles. When each side needs bigger and better weapons, it's called an arms race.

FACT: In 2010 scientists reported that they had found a new strain of bacteria in bread. It could soon be used to help keep bread fresh.

42

HUMANS AND BACTERIA ARE LOCKED IN THE SAME CONFLICT. IT'S CALLED THE EVOLUTION OF ANTIBIOTIC RESISTANCE. HERE'S AN EXAMPLE OF HOW IT WORKS:

A person becomes infected with the bacteria that cause tuberculosis. Some of these bacteria have small differences, such as a thicker cell wall. These bacteria are a different strain than the other bacteria.

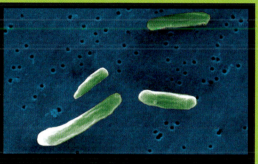

The doctor prescribes an antibiotic for the patient. The antibiotic kills all of the bacteria of one strain but not the other. The tiny differences in the strain that remains make it resistant. Almost all the infection is gone, and the patient feels better.

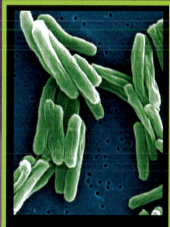

But with the other strain gone, the resistant one spreads.

The patient gets sick again. The doctor tries another drug. If it doesn't work, a new antibiotic may need to be developed.

Staying Well

Even though the risk of a pandemic is real, there's no need to live in fear of one. Every day thousands of workers around the world are tracking disease and finding ways to keep us safe. There are also many things you can do to stay well.

AVOID INFECTION: Wash your hands often. Avoid touching your eyes, nose, and mouth. Sneeze and cough into a tissue or your sleeve. Do your best to steer clear of sick people.

EAT RIGHT: Eating a healthy diet will help keep your immune system strong. Be sure to eat a variety of fruits and vegetables. A healthy diet also includes dairy products and whole grains like brown rice and whole wheat bread. Also add lean proteins such as fish, beans, eggs, and nuts to your diet.

EXERCISE: Exercise can also help strengthen your immune system. Walking to school, playing sports, or riding a bicycle are all great ways to be active. Set a goal for an hour of activity each day.

Get Enough Sleep:

Sleeping helps your body recover after working all day. Try to get at least 8 or 9 hours of sleep each night.

Stay Informed:

If there is an outbreak of disease in your area, pay attention. Listen to TV news reports, read newspapers, or look up reliable news Web sites.

Listen to Your Doctor:

If you do get sick, follow your doctor's advice. If you are prescribed a medication, follow all the instructions that came with it. It is especially important to take all of the antibiotics prescribed.

GLOSSARY

antibiotic (an-tee-by-AH-tik)—a drug that kills bacteria

antibody (AN-ti-bah-dee)—a substance produced by white blood cells that fights infections and diseases

bacterium (bak-TEER-ee-uhm)—a one-celled microbe that can cause disease or be helpful; bacteria exist in and on all living things

bioterrorism (by-oh-TER-ur-i-zuhm)—attacking with bacteria, viruses, or other disease-causing agents

dehydration (dee-hy-DRAY-shuhn)—a life-threatening medical condition caused by a lack of water

DNA—the molecule that carries the instructions to make a living thing and keep it working; DNA stands for deoxyribonucleic acid

epidemic (e-puh-DE-mik)—an outbreak of an infectious disease that affects a large number of people in a relatively small geographic area at the same time, such as in a community, region, or state

microbe (MYE-krobe)—a tiny living thing too small to be seen without a microscope

protozoan (pro-tuh-ZOH-uhn)—a small, single-celled living thing that has at least one nucleus and can be animal-like or plantlike

RNA—a molecule that contains ribose and controls certain chemical processes in a cell; RNA stands for ribonucleic acid

symptom (SIMP-tuhm) — a sign of an illness

vaccination (vak-suh-NAY-shun)—a shot of dead or weakened germs injected into a person or animal to provide protection against a disease; the dead or weakened germ is called a vaccine

virus (VYE-russ)—a disease-causing microbe with a simple structure that depends on infecting other cells to reproduce

READ MORE

Ballard, Carol. *AIDS and Other Epidemics.* What If We Do Nothing? Pleasantville, N.Y.: Gareth Stevens Pub., 2009.

Biskup, Agnieszka. *Understanding Viruses with Max Axiom, Super Scientist.* Graphic Science. Mankato, Minn.: Capstone Press, 2009.

Ollhoff, Jim. *The Germ Detectives.* A History of Germs. Edina, Minn.: ABDO Pub. Co., 2010.

Stille, Darlene R. *Outbreak!: The Science of Pandemics.* Headline Science. Mankato, Minn.: Compass Point Books, 2011.

INTERNET SITES

FactHound offers a safe, fun way to find Internet sites related to this book. All of the sites on FactHound have been researched by our staff.

Here's all you do:

Visit *www.facthound.com*

Type in this code: 9781429654937

INDEX

aid organizations, 39
alert systems, 35, 36
animals, 16, 17, 18, 24, 30, 35, 40–41
anthrax, 17, 19, 33
antibiotic resistance, 42–43
antibiotics, 27, 37, 42–43, 45
antibodies, 28

bacteria, 18–19, 20, 24, 31, 32, 33, 42, 43
B cells, 29
bioterrorism, 33
bloodletting, 13
bubonic plague, 6, 8, 11, 12, 13, 16, 19, 24, 27, 33, 38

Centers for Disease Control and Prevention (CDC), 34, 35
cholera, 8, 9, 11, 12, 17, 19, 25, 32, 39

disease prevention, 36–37, 44–45
DNA, 18, 20
doctors, 10, 13, 15, 20, 27, 30, 34, 43, 45

ecologists, 30
environmental scientists, 32
epidemics, 5, 30, 33, 34, 40
epidemiologists, 32

H1N1 influenza, 6, 27, 34, 36, 37

immune system, 10, 26, 44

Jenner, Edward, 15, 18

Koch, Robert, 17, 18

Leeuwenhoek, Anton van, 14, 18

malaria, 6, 22–23, 24, 27, 30
microbiologists, 31

outbreaks, 4, 5, 6, 9, 32, 35, 36, 39, 45

Pasteur, Louis, 16, 18
polio, 9, 10
prions, 40
protozoans, 22–23, 31

religious beliefs, 12, 13
RNA, 20
Roosevelt, Franklin D., 9

Simond, Paul-Louis, 16
smallpox, 7, 11, 13, 15, 21
Snow, Dr. John, 32
Spanish flu, 8, 38
stages of disease, 26–27
symptoms, 4, 10–11, 21, 23, 26, 27, 30

T cells, 29
tuberculosis, 10, 12, 17, 19, 43
typhoid fever, 16, 19
typhus, 7, 10, 19

U.S. Department of Homeland Security, 33

vaccinations, 9, 15, 16, 31, 37
vaccines. *See* vaccinations
vectors, 22–23, 24
　fleas, 16, 24
　mosquitoes, 22–23, 24, 30, 40
virologists, 31
viruses, 9, 10, 15, 18, 20–21, 24, 31

World Health Organization (WHO), 9, 27, 34–35, 39

yellow fever, 24

48